Empowering Leadership
Leading with Vision, Trust, and Teamwork

by Angela Boone

© Copyright. 2024 by Angela Boone

All rights reserved. No part of this publication may be reproduced, stored in a retrieval system, or transmitted in any form or by any means, electronic, mechanical, photocopying, or otherwise, without the copyright owner's prior permission.

The opinions and ideas presented in this book are solely those of the author.

Table of Contents

Introduction	4
Chapter 1: The Foundations of Great Leadership	9
Chapter 2: Leadership vs. Micro-Management	15
Chapter 3: Building Trust and Credibility	20
Chapter 4: The Art of Effective Communication	25
Chapter 5: Empowering Your Team	29
Chapter 6: Fostering Innovation and Creativity	34
Chapter 7: Leading Through Change	39
Chapter 8: The Power of Teamwork	44
Chapter 9: Developing Future Leaders	49
Chapter 10: Overcoming Insecurity	54
Conclusion	59

Introduction

Welcome to the world of leadership, where the journey is as thrilling as it is rewarding! Introducing "Empowering Leadership: Leading with Vision, Trust, and Teamwork," the comprehensive follow-up to our popular guide, now expanded into a full-length book that delves deeper into the essential strategies for effective leadership.

Leadership isn't just about holding a title or sitting in a corner office. It's about stepping up, making a difference, and inspiring others to join you on an incredible adventure. Picture this: you, as a leader, are like the captain of a ship, navigating through both calm waters and turbulent storms, always steering towards success with a crew that trusts and believes in you.

In today's dynamic workplace, leadership means more than just checking off tasks and managing people. It means being a visionary who can see beyond the horizon, an empathetic guide who understands the needs and aspirations of their team, and a flexible strategist who can adapt to change with grace. It's about creating a space where everyone feels valued, motivated, and ready to give their best.

Welcome to the book Empowering Leadership: Leading with Vision, Trust, and Teamwork. This isn't your typical leadership manual. It's a vibrant, engaging book that will transform you from a manager into a true leader. We're talking about what makes great leaders stand out: integrity, empathy, and the magical ability to inspire. We'll also tackle the dark side of leadership—micromanagement—and show you why it's the villain in our story.

Micromanagement is like trying to drive a car with the handbrake on. It stifles creativity, crushes motivation, and erodes trust. We'll explore why leaders fall into this trap and, more importantly, how to break free and empower your team to soar to new heights.

Trust is the glue that holds any great team together. It's the secret ingredient that fosters open communication, sparks innovation, and builds a sense of safety and belonging. We'll share the recipe for building and maintaining trust—transparency, consistency, and accountability—so you can inspire your team to achieve the extraordinary.

Communication is another cornerstone of stellar leadership. Imagine being a maestro, orchestrating a symphony of voices, ideas, and feedback. We'll teach you how to convey your vision with clarity, listen with empathy, and create a culture of open dialogue where every team member feels heard and valued.

Empowering your team isn't just about delegating tasks; it's about nurturing growth, providing the right resources, and creating opportunities for everyone to shine. Empowered employees are more innovative, proactive, and committed to the organization's success. We'll show you strategies for setting clear expectations, offering continuous feedback, and fostering a supportive environment that encourages personal and professional development.

Innovation and creativity are the lifeblood of any thriving organization. Great leaders cultivate a culture where team members feel safe to experiment, take risks, and share their ideas. We'll explore how to encourage collaboration and leverage diverse perspectives to drive innovative solutions and superior decision-making.

Change is inevitable, but with the right leadership, it can be an opportunity for growth rather than a source of stress. Leading through change requires a clear vision, effective communication, and a knack for managing both the emotional and practical aspects of transitions. We'll provide you with tools and strategies to navigate change smoothly and keep your team motivated and strong, recovering quickly from difficult conditions.

Teamwork makes the dream work! When individuals come together, combining their unique strengths and perspectives, the results can be phenomenal. We'll show you how to build and lead effective teams, from fostering a culture of collaboration to resolving conflicts and celebrating successes.

Finally, we'll discuss the importance of developing future leaders. By identifying and nurturing potential within your team, you can ensure a legacy of capable leaders ready to take on new challenges. We'll also guide you on mentoring and supporting emerging leaders, equipping them with the skills and confidence to succeed.

"Empowering Leadership: Leading with Vision, Trust, and Teamwork" is your comprehensive guide to becoming a more effective, inspiring, and empowering leader. Whether you're a seasoned executive or a new manager, the insights and strategies in this book will help you build a motivated, high-performing team ready to achieve extraordinary results. Let's embark on this exciting journey together!

Chapter 1
The Foundations of Great Leadership

Understanding Leadership is often perceived as a role or a position, but at its core, it is far more than that. Outstanding leadership is a blend of vision, integrity, empathy, and the ability to inspire and empower others. Understanding what makes a great leader is the first step toward becoming one. In this chapter, we will explore the essential elements of leadership and how you can develop these qualities to guide and influence those around you effectively.

Leadership is the art of motivating a group of people to act toward achieving a common goal. This definition encapsulates the essence of leadership: it is about action, influence, and purpose. Leaders are not just figureheads; they are catalysts for change, driving their teams toward success by setting a clear vision and providing the necessary support and resources to achieve it.

Great leaders have a clear vision of where they want to go and what they want to achieve. This vision serves as a guiding star for their team, providing direction and purpose. Visionary leaders are forward thinkers who anticipate challenges and opportunities, and they communicate their vision compellingly to inspire others.

Great leaders have integrity; this is the foundation of trust, which is crucial for effective leadership. Leaders with integrity are honest, ethical, and consistent in their actions and decisions. They lead by example, demonstrating the values and principles they expect from their team members.

Empathy is the ability to understand and share the feelings of others. Empathetic leaders are attuned to the needs and emotions of their team members, fostering a supportive and inclusive environment. Empathy leaders build solid and loyal relationships and enhance team cohesion by showing genuine concern for their team's well-being.

Great leaders inspire their teams to achieve more than they thought possible. They use their passion, enthusiasm, and charisma to motivate others. Inspirational leaders communicate a compelling vision and instill a sense of purpose, encouraging their team to strive for excellence and overcome obstacles.

Effective leaders are decisive and able to make timely and informed decisions. They gather and analyze relevant information, consider various perspectives, and take calculated risks. Decisiveness instills confidence in their team, as members trust their leader's ability to navigate challenges and seize opportunities.

The ability to adapt to changing circumstances is a critical quality for leaders. In today's fast-paced world, leaders must be flexible and open to new ideas and approaches. Adaptable leaders embrace change, learn from setbacks, and continuously seek improvement.

Clear and effective communication is vital for leadership. Great leaders are excellent communicators who listen actively, articulate their vision clearly, and provide constructive feedback. They foster an open communication culture, encouraging team members to share ideas and concerns.

Becoming a great leader requires continuous self-improvement and a commitment to personal and professional growth. Here are some strategies to develop and enhance your leadership skills:

Regularly assess your strengths and areas for improvement. Reflect on your experiences, seek feedback from others, and set personal development goals. Self-awareness is the first step towards becoming a more effective leader.

Stay informed about leadership theories, trends, and best practices. Read books, attend workshops, and seek mentorship from experienced leaders. Embrace a growth mindset and be open to learning from both successes and failures.

Cultivate strong relationships with your team members, peers, and mentors. Networking and building a support system can provide valuable insights, advice, and opportunities for collaboration.

Leadership skills are best developed through practice. Take on leadership roles in various settings, whether in your workplace, community, or volunteer organizations. Learn from real-life challenges and apply your knowledge in practical situations.

Encourage feedback from your team and peers to gain different perspectives on your leadership style and effectiveness. Constructive feedback can help you identify blind spots and areas for growth.

Seek out mentors who can guide and support your leadership journey. Mentors can provide valuable advice, share experiences, and help you navigate complex situations.

Outstanding leadership is a journey, not a destination. It requires a deep understanding of the fundamental qualities that define a leader and a commitment to continuous personal and professional development. By cultivating visionary thinking, integrity, empathy, inspirational influence, decisiveness, adaptability, and communication skills, you can lay the foundations for great leadership. Remember, leadership inspires and empowers others to achieve a common goal. Remember these principles as you move through your leadership journey: strive to lead with purpose, passion, and integrity.

Chapter 2
Leadership vs. Micro-Management

This is the tale of two managers. Once upon a time, in a bustling city, two managers, Emily and Steve, led teams at a dynamic marketing firm. Emily and Steve were both ambitious and driven, but their leadership styles couldn't have been more different.

Emily, known for her vibrant and energetic personality, believed in empowering her team. She saw her role as a guide and mentor, helping her team members grow and succeed. On the other hand, Steve, though equally dedicated, had a reputation for being a micro-manager. He believed the only way to ensure success was to control every detail of his team's work.

Micro-management is like trying to play all the instruments in an orchestra yourself. Steve's approach involved excessive control and involvement in the minute details of his employees' work. He constantly checked their progress, revised their work, and rarely delegated decision-making. While this style of management was intended to maintain high standards, it often led to reduced morale and productivity among his team members. Steve's micro-management had several negative effects on his team:

With Steve watching their every move, his team felt constrained. They hesitated to think creatively or take the initiative because they knew their ideas would be second-guessed. Instead of brainstorming innovative solutions, they stuck to safe, predictable paths that wouldn't attract too much scrutiny.

Steve's constant oversight made his team feel distrusted and undervalued. They felt like cogs in a machine rather than skilled professionals. The lack of trust eroded their confidence and sense of ownership over their work.

The team's motivation dwindled under Steve's relentless supervision. His constant corrections and lack of autonomy demoralized them. They began to see their work as mere tasks to be completed rather than opportunities to excel. Their joy and enthusiasm for their jobs evaporated, leaving a sense of frustration and disillusionment.

Meanwhile, Emily's leadership style was a breath of fresh air. She understood the importance of empowering her team and fostering an environment of trust and collaboration. Here's how she did it:

Emily believed in her team's abilities. She knew each member brought unique strengths to the table and trusted them to make decisions. Instead of hovering, she gave them the independence they needed to thrive. This trust empowered her team to take ownership of their projects and confidently innovate.

Emily was clear about her expectations from the start. She defined goals and provided the necessary context for each project. Once her team understood the objectives, she stepped back and allowed them the freedom to achieve them in their own way. This clarity and autonomy drove her team to exceed expectations and deliver exceptional results.

Emily was always available for guidance and support but avoided hovering over every task. She created a safe space where her team felt comfortable seeking advice and feedback. This approach encouraged open communication and collaboration, fostering a sense of community and mutual respect.

The difference between Emily's and Steve's teams was striking. Emily's team thrived under her leadership. They were motivated, creative, and felt valued. Their productivity soared, and they often came up with innovative solutions that set the company apart from its competitors. The atmosphere in Emily's team was one of camaraderie and excitement, where everyone was eager to contribute and grow.

On the other hand, Steve's team struggled. Their morale was low, and their output was lackluster. The constant oversight stifled their creativity and motivation, leading to high turnover rates and a lack of enthusiasm. The stress and frustration were palpable, and it reflected in their work.

The tale of Emily and Steve illustrates the profound impact of leadership on a team. While micro-management might seem like a way to maintain control and ensure quality, it often backfires, leading to demoralized and disengaged employees. In contrast, empowering leadership builds trust, fosters innovation, and drives exceptional performance.

By shifting from micro-management to empowerment, leaders can unlock their team's full potential. Trusting your team, setting clear expectations, and providing support without hovering are key steps to creating a thriving, motivated, and high-performing team. As leaders, it's our responsibility to guide, inspire, and empower our teams to achieve great things. Let's embrace the adventure of leadership and steer our ships toward a horizon filled with success and fulfillment.

Chapter 3
Building Trust and Credibility

The Bedrock of Leadership. Building trust and credibility is the bedrock of leadership. Imagine this: you've just been promoted to lead a new team at a cutting-edge tech startup. The atmosphere is buzzing with excitement, but there's also a hint of skepticism in the air. Your mission? To build a foundation of trust and credibility that will transform your team into a powerhouse of collaboration and innovation.

This is why trust is important. Trust is the cornerstone of a productive and positive work environment. Without it, communication breaks down, collaboration falters, and the entire team's performance suffers. Think of trust as the glue that holds everything together, allowing ideas to flow freely and teams to work harmoniously toward their goals.

Let's move forward with how you can build this essential foundation with your new team. As we all know, in everything we do, we need consistency, and the first step we will take here is priority because priority will establish consistency. Picture yourself as a lighthouse, providing a steady, reliable beacon for your team to follow. Your actions and decisions need to be predictable and dependable. If you promise to review a project by Friday, ensure it's done by Friday. When your team knows they can count on you, it creates a sense of security that's crucial for building trust.

Next, embrace transparency. Imagine having a conversation with your team where you openly share information and explain the reasoning behind your decisions. Whether it's discussing the company's direction or the rationale for a new project strategy, transparency demystifies leadership and brings everyone onto the same page. It shows your team that you value their understanding and involvement, strengthening their trust in your leadership.

Now, let's talk about accountability. Picture this scenario: a project deadline is missed, and rather than pointing fingers, you take responsibility for your part in the delay and encourage your team to do the same. Owning your mistakes motivates your team to learn from theirs, and you foster a culture of honesty and continuous improvement. Accountability isn't about assigning blame; it's about building accountability and a trust-filled environment where everyone is committed to collective success.

Building trust is just the beginning; however, maintaining credibility ensures it endures. Let's explore how you can achieve this.

First, focus on expertise. Imagine yourself as a mentor who continuously develops one's skills and knowledge. Whether staying updated with the latest industry trends or mastering new technologies, your expertise becomes a valuable resource for your team. When your team sees that you're knowledgeable and capable, they will trust your guidance and decisions more.

Honesty is paramount. Picture a problematic situation where delivering bad news is unavoidable. Instead of sugar-coating or deflecting, you choose to be honest with your team. You explain the problem clearly and discuss the steps needed to move forward. This level of honesty, even when it's tough, shows your team that you respect them and are committed to transparency, further solidifying their trust in you.

Finally, let's consider fairness. Imagine a team member approaching you with a concern about workload distribution. Instead of dismissing their worry, you listen attentively and take steps to ensure everyone is treated equally and respectfully. Fairness in your decisions and interactions fosters an environment where all team members feel valued and respected, which is essential for maintaining long-term trust and credibility.

As you navigate your leadership journey, remember that trust and credibility are not just built overnight. They are cultivated through consistent actions, transparent communication, accountable leadership, continuous expertise, honesty, and fairness. By embodying these principles, you create a solid foundation for your team to thrive.

Your team, once skeptical, now looks up to you as a leader they can trust and rely on. The office buzzes with positive energy, ideas flow freely, and collaboration reaches new heights. Trust, after all, is the bedrock of any successful team, and with it firmly in place, there's no limit to what you can achieve together.

So, set sail on this exciting leadership adventure, armed with the tools to build trust and credibility. Your team's success is bound to follow, driven by the strong foundation you've laid. Here's to a journey filled with trust, respect, and incredible achievements!

Chapter 4
The Art of Effective Communication

There are many keys to the art of effective communication, which we will touch on in this chapter. Let's start with the symphony of leadership when it comes to the role of communication. Picture this: you're conducting a symphony where every instrument must play in harmony to create a beautiful piece of music. This is the essence of effective communication in leadership. It's the art of conveying vision, building relationships, and resolving conflicts seamlessly. Communication isn't just about talking; it's about creating a flow of understanding that binds your team together, driving them toward a shared goal.

Effective communication is the lifeblood of successful leadership. Imagine navigating a ship through uncharted waters without clear instructions – chaos, right? Similarly, without effective communication, your team can't align with your vision, understand their roles, or feel connected to the mission. Communication ensures everyone is on the same page, working collaboratively and efficiently.

Active listening is one of the critical key skills that begins communication magic. Imagine a team member approaching you with a new idea. Instead of waiting for your turn to speak, you genuinely listen to understand their perspective. This means paying attention, asking clarifying questions, and acknowledging their points. Active listening shows respect and fosters an environment where team members feel valued and heard.

Clarity is the backbone of effective communication. Imagine giving your team a complex project brief. If your instructions are muddled or ambiguous, you'll likely be confused and make mistakes. Clear and concise communication ensures that your team knows exactly what's expected of them. It eliminates guesswork and streamlines execution.

Empathy is the bridge that connects you to your team on a deeper level. Imagine one of your team members is struggling with a personal issue. Showing understanding and consideration for their feelings and perspectives builds trust and rapport. Empathy allows you to support your team effectively, fostering a positive and inclusive work environment.

Regular updates are essential for keeping your team informed and engaged. Imagine holding weekly check-ins where you discuss goals, progress, and any changes. These updates ensure everyone is aligned and aware of their roles and responsibilities. It's like having a roadmap that guides your team toward their objectives, keeping them focused and motivated.

This is important; an open-door policy encourages open communication and makes you accessible to your team. However, ensure your open-door policy is not for a select few but your entire team. Picture your team members knowing they can come to you with ideas, concerns, or feedback anytime. This openness fosters a culture of transparency and trust. It breaks down barriers and encourages candid conversations, leading to more innovative solutions and stronger team cohesion.

Fostering a feedback culture where constructive feedback is valued is crucial for continuous improvement. Imagine regularly giving and receiving feedback that's aimed at growth and development. This culture promotes accountability and learning, helping your team to refine their skills and performance continuously. When given thoughtfully, feedback can be a powerful tool for personal and professional growth.

Effective communication is more than just a skill; it's an ongoing practice that enhances every aspect of leadership. By mastering active listening, clarity, and empathy and implementing strategies like regular updates, an open-door policy, and a feedback culture, you can transform the way your team operates.

Your team will become well-oiled and rounded individuals where everyone knows their role, feels valued, and is motivated to contribute their best. Most conflicts are resolved smoothly, ideas flow freely, and the collective energy drives you toward success. Communication is the symphony that brings all the instruments of leadership together, creating a harmonious and powerful performance.

So, embrace the art of effective communication and watch your leadership journey soar. With these tools, you'll convey your vision and build strong relationships and navigate challenges gracefully and easily. Here's to leading with clarity, empathy, and confidence!

Chapter 5
Empowering Your Team

The Power of Empowerment leads to job satisfaction, higher productivity, and more significant innovation. Imagine you're the captain of a vibrant, bustling ship. You've charted the course and set the destination, and now it's time to let your crew take the helm. This is the essence of empowerment in leadership. Empowering your team is not just about delegating tasks; it's about creating an environment where everyone feels capable, confident, and motivated to contribute their best. It's like unlocking a treasure chest of potential that leads to job satisfaction, higher productivity, and greater innovation.

The importance of empowerment is the secret sauce that transforms a good team into a great one. Employees who feel empowered take ownership of their work, bring creative solutions, and are more engaged in their roles. Think of empowerment as giving your team the keys to the kingdom – they feel trusted, valued, and ready to tackle any challenge. This sense of ownership leads to higher job satisfaction, as team members feel their contributions make a meaningful impact. It also boosts productivity and innovation, as empowered employees are likelier to take initiative and think outside the box.

There are many ways to empower your team, and delegation is the cornerstone of empowerment. Imagine you're preparing for a big project. Instead of micromanaging every detail, you assign responsibilities to your team members, trusting them to deliver. Delegation is not just about offloading tasks; it's about entrusting your team with meaningful responsibilities that match their skills and interests. By doing so, you show that you believe in their abilities, which boosts their confidence and encourages them to take ownership of their work. When team members feel trusted, they are more likely to go above and beyond to achieve their goals.

Encouragement is another way to empower your team; it's the wind in your team's sails. Picture a team member coming up with a bold, new idea. Instead of shooting it down, you encourage them to take the risk and explore it further. Encouraging risk-taking and supporting your team in their efforts creates a culture of innovation and continuous improvement. It's about creating a safe environment where failure is seen as a learning opportunity rather than a setback. When your team feels supported in taking risks, they are more likely to experiment and innovate, leading to groundbreaking solutions and progress.

Development opportunities are another way to empower your team; they are the building blocks of a skilled and motivated team. Imagine offering your team workshops, training sessions, and mentorship programs. Providing opportunities for professional growth and development not only enhances their skills but also shows that you are invested in their future. This investment pays off over time, as team members feel valued and motivated to apply their new skills. Development opportunities also pave the way for career advancement, which keeps your team engaged and committed to their roles.

Another way to empower your team is the ripple effect. The ripple effect of empowerment is transformative. When you empower your team, you create a positive, dynamic work environment where everyone is motivated to contribute their best. Empowered employees are more satisfied with their jobs, leading to higher retention rates and a more stable, experienced team. They are also more productive, feeling a sense of ownership and responsibility for their work. This productivity translates to better performance and greater results for your organization.

Innovation flourishes in an empowered team. When team members are encouraged to take risks and supported in their efforts, they are more likely to think creatively and come up with innovative solutions. This culture of innovation drives continuous improvement and keeps your organization at the cutting edge of your industry.

Empowering your team is not a one-time effort; it's a continuous practice that enhances every aspect of your leadership. By mastering delegation, providing encouragement, and offering development opportunities, you can unlock the full potential of your team. Your role as a leader is to create an environment where everyone feels capable, confident, and motivated to contribute their best.

As your team feels empowered, you'll notice a significant boost in job satisfaction, productivity, and innovation. The workplace becomes a vibrant, dynamic environment where everyone is eager to collaborate, share ideas, and drive the organization forward. Empowerment is the key to transforming your team and achieving extraordinary results.

So, embrace the power of empowerment and watch your team soar. With these tools, you'll create a motivated, high-performing team ready to tackle any challenge and achieve incredible success. Here's to leading with trust, encouragement, and a commitment to continuous growth!

Chapter 6
Fostering Innovation and Creativity

The Magic of Innovation. Imagine entering a workspace buzzing with excitement, where ideas bounce off the walls, and creativity flows like an unstoppable river. This is the magic of an innovative environment. When you foster innovation and creativity, you unleash the potential for extraordinary problem-solving and performance. It's like turning your team into a group of fearless explorers, ready to chart new territories and discover groundbreaking solutions.

An innovative environment is a fertile ground for creativity and problem-solving. It's where the seeds of new ideas are planted and nurtured until they blossom into game-changing solutions. This kind of environment doesn't just happen; it's cultivated through deliberate actions and an open mindset. When you create an innovative environment, you empower your team to think differently, take risks, and push the boundaries of what's possible.

As a leader, you must be open-minded; open-mindedness is the gateway to creativity. Imagine holding a brainstorming session where no idea is too wild or outlandish. Being open to new ideas and different perspectives is crucial for fostering creativity. Encourage your team to think outside the box and challenge the status quo. When team members feel their unique viewpoints are valued, they're more likely to share their most creative ideas. This diversity of thought can lead to innovative solutions that you might never have considered.

Collaboration is another way that drives innovation. Picture your team working together, bouncing ideas off each other, and building on each other's strengths. Foster a culture where collaboration and the sharing of ideas are the norms. Create physical and virtual spaces where team members can come together to brainstorm and problem-solve. Collaboration brings together different skill sets and perspectives, leading to richer, more creative solutions. When people work together, they can achieve far more than they could individually.

Creating an environment where it's safe to take risks and fail is essential for innovation. Imagine a lab where experiments are encouraged, and failures are seen as learning opportunities. When your team knows it's okay to fail, they're more likely to take bold risks and try new approaches. This safe-to-fail culture fosters experimentation and continuous improvement. It's important to celebrate the effort and the lessons learned from failures, not just the successes. Doing so creates an innovative team that's constantly pushing the envelope.

There are benefits of an innovative environment. An innovative environment does wonders for your team and organization. It encourages creativity and problem-solving, leading to better solutions and improved performance. Here's how:

When creativity is unleashed, problem-solving becomes more dynamic and effective. Innovative environments produce solutions that are not only unique but also highly effective. Your team learns to approach problems from multiple angles, resulting in comprehensive and innovative solutions that stand out in the market.

Innovation drives performance, and the teams that feel empowered to innovate are more engaged and motivated. They take pride in their work and are committed to finding the best solutions. This commitment translates into higher productivity and better results. An innovative environment keeps your team on their toes, always striving for excellence and continuous improvement.

An environment that fosters innovation also engages employees and increases engagement. When team members feel that their ideas matter and that they have the freedom to explore new possibilities, they're more invested in their work. This engagement leads to higher job satisfaction and retention rates. People want to be part of a team where they can grow, learn, and make a real impact.

Fostering innovation and creativity is a continuous journey that requires intentional effort and an open mindset. By embracing open-mindedness, encouraging collaboration, and creating a safe-to-fail environment, you can cultivate a culture of innovation that propels your team to new heights.

As you nurture this innovative environment, your team transforms into a powerhouse of creativity and problem-solving. The workplace will buzz with energy and excitement, and the results will speak for themselves. Your organization will be known for its innovative solutions and high performance, setting you apart in a competitive market.

So, let's go on this thrilling journey of fostering innovation and creativity together. With these tools, you'll create a dynamic, engaged team ready to tackle any challenge and achieve extraordinary success. Here's to leading with an open mind, a collaborative spirit, and the courage to embrace failure as a stepping stone to greatness!

**Chapter 7
Leading Through Change**

The Challenge of Change. Imagine standing at the edge of a vast, uncharted territory, ready to lead your team into the unknown. Change is like that—a thrilling yet daunting adventure. It can be challenging, but influential leaders navigate it smoothly by maintaining stability and guiding their teams through transitions. Embracing change isn't just about managing the process; it's about inspiring your team to see the opportunities and growth that come with it.

First and foremost, provide a clear vision of the change and the reasons behind it. Picture yourself as an explorer charting a new course. Your team needs to understand where they're headed and why it's important. By communicating the goals and benefits of the change clearly and passionately, your team will see the bigger picture and understand the purpose behind the shift; they'll be more likely to embrace it with enthusiasm. It's like giving them a map and compass to navigate the journey ahead.

Involve your team in the change process to increase buy-in. Imagine hosting a council where everyone's voice is heard and valued. When team members are involved in planning and decision-making, they feel a sense of ownership and commitment. This involvement can take many forms, from brainstorming sessions to feedback loops. By actively engaging your team, you tap into their collective wisdom and creativity, making the change process more inclusive and effective.

Provide the necessary support and resources to help your team adapt to change. Think of yourself as a guide on this expedition, ensuring everyone has the tools and support they need to succeed. This includes offering training, resources, and continuous encouragement. Address any concerns and provide solutions to obstacles they might face. Support also means being present and approachable so your team feels confident they can rely on you throughout the transition.

Leading through change is much like steering a ship through a storm. The waves and high winds are fierce, but you can guide your team to calmer waters with a steady hand and clear direction. Let's explore how these strategies play out in real-life scenarios.

Imagine your company is undergoing a major rebranding effort. As a leader, you gather your team to explain the new vision: a refreshed brand that better reflects your core values and market position. You share the story behind the change, the expected benefits, and how each team member plays a crucial role in this transformation. Your passion and clarity inspire your team, turning initial apprehension into excitement. They now see the change not as a disruption but as an exciting evolution they're eager to participate in.

Next, you involve your team in the rebranding process. You organize workshops where everyone can contribute ideas for the new brand identity. You create feedback loops where team members can voice their concerns and suggestions. This collaborative approach generates a wealth of creative ideas and fosters a sense of ownership. Your team feels valued and integral to the change, increasing their commitment and enthusiasm.

Throughout the rebranding effort, you provide continuous support. You offer training sessions on new branding tools and platforms. You set up regular check-ins to address any challenges and provide solutions. You celebrate small wins, boosting morale and keeping the momentum going. Your presence and support reassure your team that they're not alone in this journey, building their confidence and resilience.

Successfully leading through change has profound rewards. Your team emerges stronger, more cohesive, and more adaptable. They've navigated the storm together, learning valuable lessons and building trust along the way. The change, once seen as a daunting challenge, becomes a testament to your team's strength and your leadership.

An organization that can effectively navigate change thrives in any environment. Change becomes an opportunity for growth and innovation rather than a threat. Your empowered team is better equipped to handle future challenges and seize new opportunities.

Leading through change is more than just managing transitions; it's about inspiring and empowering your team to see the possibilities and embrace the journey. By providing a clear vision, involving your team, and offering unwavering support, you can turn the challenge of change into an exciting adventure.

So, set sail confidently and lead your team through the uncharted waters of change. With these strategies, you'll create a dynamic team ready to navigate any storm and emerge stronger on the other side. Here's to embracing change and leading with vision, collaboration, and support!

Chapter 8
The Power of Teamwork

The Value of Teamwork. Imagine assembling a puzzle where each piece is vital to completing the picture. Teamwork is like that puzzle; every team member's contribution is crucial to achieving the bigger goal. The power of teamwork lies in its ability to bring together diverse skills and perspectives, leading to better problem-solving, increased innovation, and improved performance. When individuals work cohesively as a team, their combined efforts create something far greater than the sum of their parts.

Teamwork is the secret ingredient that propels organizations to new heights. It fosters a collaborative environment where creativity and innovation thrive. When team members share a common goal and work together to achieve it, they can tackle complex problems more effectively and generate innovative solutions that might not be possible individually. Additionally, a strong team enhances performance by leveraging each member's strengths and compensating for their weaknesses, leading to higher productivity and better results.

Building a strong team ensures that everyone is aligned with shared goals. Picture a rowing team moving in perfect sync towards the finish line. It's essential that all team members understand the overarching objectives and how their individual roles contribute to achieving them. Clear, shared goals create a sense of purpose and direction, motivating everyone to work together harmoniously.

Encouraging collaboration is key to unlocking your team's full potential. Imagine a brainstorming session where ideas flow freely and everyone feels comfortable contributing. Collaboration brings diverse perspectives to the table, fostering creativity and innovation. Create an environment where team members can openly share their ideas and build on each other's thoughts. This collaborative spirit not only leads to better solutions but also strengthens the bonds within the team.

Fostering a mutual respect and trust culture is the bedrock of effective teamwork. Picture a team where everyone feels valued and respected for their contributions. Trust is built through consistent actions, open communication, and mutual support. When team members trust and respect each other, they are more likely to collaborate effectively, take risks, and support one another, leading to a more cohesive and productive team.

Team-building activities are like the glue that binds a team together. Imagine organizing a fun retreat where team members engage in activities that strengthen their relationships and improve collaboration. These activities can range from problem-solving challenges to social outings, helping team members build rapport and trust. Team-building activities create a positive and cohesive team culture, enhancing overall performance.

As a leader, ensuring that everyone knows their role and responsibilities is crucial for effective teamwork. Picture a football team where each player knows their position and responsibilities on the field. Clearly defined roles eliminate confusion, reduce overlaps, and ensure everyone is focused on their tasks. This clarity enables the team to function smoothly and efficiently, maximizing productivity and performance.

Sometimes, there will still be a little conflict in everything we do. However, addressing conflicts quickly and fairly is essential to maintaining team harmony. Imagine a team where disagreements are resolved constructively, leading to better understanding and collaboration. Conflict is inevitable, but how it's managed makes all the difference. Encourage open communication and provide a safe space for team members to express their concerns. Addressing conflicts promptly and fairly prevents them from escalating and ensures that the team remains focused and united.

The impact of teamwork extends far beyond achieving immediate goals. It builds a strong foundation for long-term success by creating a supportive and collaborative work environment. Teams that work well together are more adaptable and better equipped to handle challenges and seize opportunities. The sense of shared purpose boosts morale, job satisfaction, and retention rates, creating a positive and productive workplace.

The power of teamwork is undeniable. By building a strong team with shared goals, fostering collaboration, and creating a culture of respect and trust, you can harness your team's collective potential. Implementing teamwork strategies like team-building activities, clear roles and responsibilities, and effective conflict resolution further strengthens the team's performance.

As you cultivate a collaborative, supportive team environment, you'll see your team tackle challenges with creativity, innovate continuously, and achieve exceptional results. Teamwork transforms individual efforts into collective success, driving your organization forward.

So, embrace the power of teamwork and watch your team thrive. With these strategies, you'll create a dynamic, high-performing team ready to conquer any challenge and achieve extraordinary success. Here's to leading with shared goals, collaboration, respect, and trust!

Chapter 9
Developing Future Leaders

The Importance of Developing Leaders. Imagine a thriving garden where each plant is carefully nurtured to reach its full potential. Developing future leaders within your organization is much like tending to that garden. It ensures your organization's continued success and growth by cultivating a pipeline of talented individuals ready to step into leadership roles. When you invest in developing leaders, you're not just preparing for the future; you're creating a dynamic organization capable of navigating any challenge.

The first step in developing future leaders is identifying those with potential. Picture yourself as a talent scout, always on the lookout for individuals who demonstrate leadership qualities and a willingness to take on responsibility. These individuals often stand out through their initiative, problem-solving skills, and ability to inspire and influence others. Observing how team members handle challenges, interact with their peers, and contribute to projects can reveal who is ready for more significant responsibilities.

Once you've identified potential leaders, the next step is mentorship. Imagine yourself as a seasoned guide, sharing your wisdom and experience with a protégé. Providing mentorship and guidance helps potential leaders develop their skills and gain confidence. This relationship allows for personalized support, where you can offer advice, feedback, and encouragement tailored to their unique strengths and areas for growth. Through mentorship, you create a supportive environment that fosters personal and professional development.

Once you have identified potential leaders, it's time to develop a "Leadership Development Program." This can involve training programs and workshops.

Training programs and workshops are essential tools for developing leadership skills. Picture a series of dynamic, interactive sessions where employees can learn, practice, and refine their leadership abilities. These programs should cover various topics, from effective communication and decision-making to conflict resolution and strategic thinking. Offering training and workshops equips potential leaders with the necessary skills and demonstrates your commitment to their growth and development.

Providing opportunities for employees to take on leadership roles and responsibilities is crucial for their development and the growth and future of the company. Imagine giving a promising team member the chance to lead a project or manage a small team. These opportunities allow potential leaders to gain hands-on experience and apply what they've learned in real-world scenarios. It's like giving them the reins of a powerful racehorse, allowing them to harness their potential and prove their capabilities. By gradually increasing their responsibilities, you help them build confidence and competence as leaders.

There is an impact on developing future Leaders. Developing future leaders has a profound effect on your organization. It creates a continuous growth and improvement culture where employees feel valued and motivated to advance their careers. This investment in leadership development also ensures that your organization has a steady supply of capable leaders ready to step up when needed, reducing the risk of leadership gaps and ensuring seamless transitions.

Moreover, a focus on developing leaders fosters a sense of loyalty and engagement among employees. They see that the organization is committed to their professional growth, which boosts morale and retention rates. This dedication to nurturing talent also enhances your organization's reputation, attracting top-tier candidates who want to be part of a company that invests in its people.

The journey of developing future leaders is an ongoing process that requires dedication, observation, mentorship, and structured development programs. By identifying potential leaders, providing mentorship, and offering training and growth opportunities, you create a robust leadership pipeline that secures your organization's future success.

As you nurture and develop these future leaders, you'll witness a transformation within your organization. Employees will be more engaged, motivated, and prepared to take on new challenges. Your organization will thrive, driven by a team of capable leaders ready to innovate and lead with confidence.

So, embark on this exciting journey of developing future leaders. With these strategies, you'll cultivate a vibrant garden of talent, ensuring your organization's continued growth and success. Here's to leading with vision, mentorship, and a commitment to nurturing the leaders of tomorrow!

Chapter 10
Overcoming Insecurity

The Hidden Threat of Insecurity. Imagine being the captain of a ship, and you spot a rising star among your crew—someone with exceptional skills and potential. But instead of celebrating this talent, you feel insecure, fearing they might one day take your job. This scenario is more common than you think and can be a hidden threat to effective leadership and organizational success. As a leader, it's crucial to recognize and overcome these prejudices to excel and foster a thriving work environment.

Great leaders understand that the true measure of their success lies in their ability to develop and elevate others. Recognizing talent, irrespective of race or gender, and not being intimidated by it is a hallmark of exceptional leadership. If you let insecurities dictate your actions, you're not only stifling the potential of others but also jeopardizing the organization's future. Here's why seeing potential in others and fostering it is crucial:

Imagine a basketball coach who refuses to put the best player on the court because of personal insecurities. The team's performance suffers, and so does morale. Similarly, when leaders are intimidated by talented individuals in the workplace, they hinder the team's overall strength and success. Embracing and nurturing talent, on the other hand, builds a stronger, more capable team, ready to tackle challenges and innovate.

Authentic leadership isn't about maintaining power but about empowering others. Imagine a leader who celebrates the achievements of their team members, regardless of their own insecurities. This attitude inspires loyalty and respect and sets a powerful example for the entire organization. Demonstrating authentic leadership encourages a culture of growth, collaboration, and mutual respect.

Holding back talented individuals out of fear can have dire consequences for the organization. It's like a gardener refusing to water the strongest plants, leading to a withered garden. When leaders fail to recognize and develop talent, they stifle innovation and progress, potentially causing the organization to stagnate or even decline. Embracing and fostering talent, however, ensures continuous growth and adaptation in a competitive landscape.

The first step in overcoming these insecurities is self-awareness. Imagine looking in a mirror and acknowledging your fears and prejudices. Reflect on why you feel threatened by certain individuals and understand that these feelings are natural but must be managed. Recognize that your role as a leader is to uplift others, not to hold them back.

Embrace your team's diversity of skills, perspectives, and experiences. Imagine a diverse orchestra where each instrument adds a unique sound, creating a beautiful symphony. By valuing and celebrating diversity, you create an inclusive environment where everyone feels valued and empowered to contribute their best.

Transform your insecurities into opportunities for growth by becoming a mentor. Imagine taking a talented team member under your wing, guiding and watching them flourish. Providing mentorship and support helps the individual grow, strengthens your leadership skills, and builds a legacy of excellence within the organization.

Failing to overcome insecurities and prejudices can have severe repercussions. Imagine a ship slowly sinking because the captain refused to allow the best sailors to navigate. When leaders are driven by insecurity, they risk creating a toxic work environment, lowering morale, and ultimately harming the organization's success. Recognizing that true leadership involves putting the organization's needs above personal fears is essential.

Overcoming prejudices and insecurities is a critical component of effective leadership. By recognizing and nurturing talent without intimidation, you build a stronger, more innovative team, demonstrate true leadership, and ensure the organization's continued growth and success. It's about creating a culture where everyone, regardless of race, gender, or background, can thrive and contribute to the collective success.

As you continue your leadership journey, remember that the true test of a leader is their ability to elevate others. Embrace the challenge, celebrate diversity, and transform insecurities into opportunities for growth. By doing so, you'll not only enhance your leadership skills but also foster a thriving, dynamic organization ready to conquer any challenge.

So, confidently lead with vision, inclusivity, and support. Here's to overcoming prejudices, empowering your team, and achieving extraordinary success together!

Conclusion

Leadership transcends the mere administration of tasks. It encompasses inspiring and empowering your team to reach their fullest potential. A true leader understands that their role is not confined to overseeing daily operations but extends to nurturing an environment where each team member feels valued and motivated.

A critical distinction lies between leadership and micro-management. Meanwhile, micro-managers focus on controlling every detail, often stifling creativity. Influential leaders provide direction and support, trusting their team to execute tasks independently. This approach fosters a sense of ownership and responsibility among team members, enhancing their performance and satisfaction.

Trust forms the cornerstone of effective leadership. Leaders build trust within their teams by demonstrating integrity, transparency, and consistency. Trust is cultivated through open communication, mutual respect, and a genuine interest in team members' well-being. When employees trust their leader, they are more likely to take initiative, voice innovative ideas, and go above and beyond in their roles.

Effective communication is paramount in leadership. It involves conveying information clearly and actively listening to team members. Leaders who communicate effectively ensure that everyone is on the same page, reducing misunderstandings and fostering a collaborative environment. Open lines of communication allow for sharing ideas, feedback, and concerns, contributing to continuous improvement and team cohesion.

Empowerment involves giving team members the resources they need to excel. Leaders who empower their teams delegate authority, provide opportunities for professional growth, and encourage decision-making at all levels. This empowerment boosts morale, increases engagement, and drives innovation, as team members feel confident in their abilities and supported in their endeavors.

Innovation thrives in an environment where creativity is encouraged and valued. Leaders play a crucial role in fostering innovation by creating a safe space for experimentation and learning from failure. By celebrating innovative ideas and rewarding creative solutions, leaders inspire their teams to think outside the box and continuously seek improvement.

Change is coming in any organization; influential leaders navigate it with foresight. Leading through change involves clear communication, empathy, and a strategic approach. Leaders must articulate the vision and rationale behind changes, address concerns, and provide support to help their team adapt. By demonstrating flexibility and a positive attitude towards change, leaders set the tone for their team to embrace new challenges and opportunities.

Teamwork is the essence of a successful organization. Leaders who promote teamwork encourage collaboration, recognize collective achievements, and build a sense of community within the team. They understand each team member's strengths and weaknesses and leverage these dynamics to achieve common goals. By fostering a culture of mutual support and cooperation, leaders enhance the team's overall performance and cohesiveness.

Investing in future leaders' development is crucial for any organization's sustained success. Great leaders mentor and coach their team members, providing guidance and opportunities for growth. By identifying and nurturing potential leaders, organizations ensure continuous growth.

Developing future leaders creates a talent pipeline ready to take on new challenges and move the organization forward.

Leadership is an art that goes beyond managing tasks; it is about inspiring, empowering, and guiding your team to achieve their best. You can cultivate a thriving organizational culture by embracing trust, effective communication, empowerment, innovation, adaptability, teamwork, and leadership development. Lead with vision, trust, and a commitment to fostering a collaborative and innovative environment, and you will achieve success and leave a lasting legacy of effective leadership.

About the Author

Angela Boone has over 35 years of experience in the construction industry and has gained deep insights into the true nature of leadership. Her extensive career, which includes working on projects ranging from modest budgets to a billion-dollar capital improvement program, has shown her that leadership transcends mere titles. Through her book "Empowering Leadership: Leading with Vision, Trust, and Teamwork"(The Full Book), Angela aims to convey that effective leadership is about more than just holding a position of authority—it's about inspiring and guiding others toward a shared vision.

Having received numerous accolades, including being named one of the top ten businesswomen of distinction by the National Association of Women Business Owners (NAWBO) and being recognized in national publications, such as Essence and Essence Special Coffee Table titled, Making It Happen, Creating Success and Abundance". The coffee table books offered readers a hard and soft cover. Angela understands leadership involves building trust, fostering teamwork, and consistently demonstrating integrity and vision. She has seen firsthand how these qualities can lead to successful project outcomes and motivated teams. Angela's book is a collection of her experiences and lessons learned, offering valuable insights and practical advice to current and aspiring leaders on truly empowering their teams and leading with authenticity and purpose.

To learn more, check out our blog at:
www.ARBooneConstruction.com

Books, eBooks and Guides

Empowering Leadership: *Leading with Vision, Trust, and Teamwork.* (The Full Book)

Empowering Leadership: *Leading with Vision, Trust, and Teamwork (*The Short Guide*)*

Be Aware of the Footprint You Leave Behind: *The Next Level Celebration – Between Mortar and Miracles: A Woman's Triumph in Construction.* (The Full Book)

Mission: Retirement - *Your Ultimate Guide to Transitioning from Military Service to Civilian Success.* (The Full Book)

I'M Retired…What's Next? - *A guide crafted especially for baby boomers who are moving or have moved into the exciting journey of retirement. This book is your companion in discovering how to leverage your incredible skills, knowledge, and experience to make a meaningful impact on the world around you.* (The Full Book)

NOTES:

www.ingramcontent.com/pod-product-compliance
Lightning Source LLC
Chambersburg PA
CBHW070121230526
45472CB00004B/1355